PRAYER AND HOLINESS

The Icon of Man Renewed in God

DUMITRU STANILOAE

SLG PRESS
Convent of the Incarnation
Fairacres Oxford

ISBN 0 7283 0093 1
ISSN 0307-1405

CONTENTS

ACKNOWLEDGEMENT

The five essays presented here were originally addresses given to the monks at the Monastery of Chevetogne in Belgium, a Benedictine community dedicated to work and pray for Christian unity, and especially for unity between Christian East and West. The addresses first appeared in 1979 in *Irénikon*, the journal of the Community, under the title: 'Bréviaire hésychaste'. The Sisters of the Love of God wish to record their gratitude to Dom Michael van Parys, the Prior of Chevetogne, for generously allowing them to publish their translation of Fr Staniloae's addresses, the first of which, 'Tenderness and Holiness', has already appeared in the *Fairacres Chronicle*, Summer 1981.

INTRODUCTION

FATHER DUMITRU STANILOAE, the author of the five essays presented in this little book, is one of the most distinguished of Orthodox theologians. Born in 1903, he has been professor of dogmatic theology both at Sibiu in Transylvania and at Bucharest, and has written many books, notable among them a three volume *Dogmatic Theology* (1978). A priest and a married man, he has throughout his life been concerned to stress the links between theology and spirituality. Hence he is also the editor of the new and enlarged Romanian version of the *Philokalia*. This great anthology of spiritual writings has in the last two hundred years played an important part in strengthening the inner life of the Orthodox Churches, in Romania no less than in Russia and Greece, and the first two volumes are now available in English.

Fr Staniloae, as we have said, has always sought to show the links between theology and spirituality. Still more has he wanted to make it clear that both are rooted in the faith and life and prayer of the whole Christian people. Hence, in the pages that follow you will find the words of an eminent scholar, an original thinker, a man of deep prayer, but also of a man who has never lost touch with the faith and experience of a great variety of people in many walks of life. Theology should be at the service of the whole Christian community, an articulation of the faith which is held by all. I remember Fr Dumitru once telling me that when thinking through some difficult theological problem, he would sometimes say to himself, 'How would the villagers at home feel about this?'

We have therefore in these pages an expression of the faith of the Church and of the experience of all her people. So, for instance, when you come to the last section you will find that the renewal of the Church is considered not as a matter for experts sitting on a commission, but in terms of your prayer and mine, our willingness to forgive and be forgiven. It is in our hands to further or hinder the progress of renewal.

It is altogether characteristic of their author that in these pages the most difficult questions are treated with the greatest simplicity. In the first section we see how the gentleness and firmness of the man of God, his power to comfort and his power to incite, his nearness and yet his distance, are all things rooted in the transcendent love of God, which comes close to us in him. Western Christians will be reminded as they read of such men as the Curé d'Ars and Bishop Edward King. In the second section we look further into the way in which, in prayer, man is carried out of himself in love for the God who has come out from himself in love for man. We find the true meaning of the ancient phrase about 'putting the mind into the heart', the union of man's faculties in their movement towards God.

The third section brings us to a consideration of the doctrines of the Incarnation and of deification. The greatest exponent of these doctrines in the Orthodox tradition is St Maximus the Confessor. Here they are expressed with a power and directness which convey something of the immensity of the love of God, the limitless possibilities of the life of man. 'Man must be capable of continually renewing and deepening his conscious experience of God; and God in his turn delights in this perpetual renewal of joy in the man in whom he rests.'

The fourth section discusses the nature of human freedom. From the thought of man's freedom as a person in relation to the natural order, it brings us to a wonderful statement of the way in which human freedom is grounded in the infinite freedom of God, who makes us free in the gift of his Holy and Life-giving Spirit.

We have already mentioned the fifth section with its stress on the need to ask and to grant forgiveness.

Mutual forgiveness of each vice
Opens the gate of Paradise.

It is important that full weight should be given to this section. This is the earth in which all the rest is planted; this simple direct confrontation with the words of the prayer which every Christian makes his own: 'Forgive us our trespasses as we forgive them that trespass against us'.

It has been an honour for the Sisters of the Love of God to translate and publish these texts in English; it is an honour for me to introduce them. May they live and work in us, and may a little of that love which animates their author in all that he does come to animate all who read and ponder them.

Feast of the Annunciation 1982 A. M. ALLCHIN

I

TENDERNESS AND HOLINESS

IN THE PERSON of the saint, because of his availability, his extreme attention to others, and by the alacrity with which he gives himself to Christ, humanity is healed and renewed. How does this renewed humanity show itself in practice? The saint shows us a bearing full of tact, transparency, purity of thought and feeling, in relation to every human being. His consideration extends even to animals and to things, because in every creature he sees a gift of God's love, and does not wish to wound that love by treating his gifts with negligence or indifference. He has respect for each man and for each thing. He shows towards the suffering of any man, or even of an animal, a profound compassion.

St Isaac the Syrian says of the compassion of the saint: 'What can one say of a soul, of a heart, filled with compassion? It is a heart which burns with love for every creature: for men, birds and animals, for serpents and for demons. The thought of them and the sight of them make the tears of the saint flow. And this immense and intense compassion, which flows from the heart of the saints, makes them unable to bear the sight of the smallest, most insignificant wound in any creature. Thus they pray ceaselessly, with tears, even for animals, for enemies of the truth and for those who do them wrong.'

As to St Callinicus of Cernica (the most recent of the canonical saints of Romania, who died in 1867), when he was in some town where he had no money to give to the poor, he would turn to his companions with tears, saying, 'Do get me some money to give to these little brothers of Jesus'.

Such compassion reveals a heart that is tender, extremely sensitive, and a stranger to all hardness, indifference and brutality. It shows us that hardness is the result of sin and of the passions. In the bearing of the saint, and even in his thoughts, there is no trace of vulgarity, meanness or baseness; no sign of affectation, or want of sincerity. Kindliness, sensitivity and transparency come to their fullest expression in him, and are combined with purity, generous attention towards men and with the availability by which he shares with all his heart in their problems and troubles. In all these qualities is shown forth in an eminent degree the full capacity of human nature.

There is indeed a distinction and nobility full of feeling in this higher form of tenderness that is very different from the conventional distinction and nobility which are distant and formal. This tenderness does not avoid contact with the most humble of men, and is unperturbed by situations in which others would be afraid of falling. The model of this tenderness is the *kenosis*, the condescension, of Christ. He did not wish to hold himself aloof from sinners, nor from the kind of women who are avoided by men concerned for their own reputation. The *kenosis*, the self-emptying of Christ is, in itself, the supreme form of tenderness. In it is shown the desire not to be a burden to the humble, not to embarrass them. By his *kenosis* he desired to open up a way into their hearts. By kindness he intended to make them give up their cruel ways, instead of persisting in a hardness in which the 'inferior' returns the contempt of the 'superior'.

In the kindliness of their behaviour the saints are inspired by the *kenosis* of Christ. At the same time they are the harbingers of a higher level of human relations in which kindness will be paramount. For humanity, still unsatisfied by the exterior equality which men are coming to realise among themselves, is tending towards a higher level of mutual relationships which will bear the marks of tenderness.

Thanks to a conscience whose sensitivity has been nourished and refined by the sensitivity of God made man for men, a sensitivity in which they share, the saints can see into the most secret states of soul in others, and they avoid anything that could be a stumbling-block to them without, however, neglecting to help them triumph over their weaknesses and conquer their difficulties. Thus the saint is sought out as a confidant for the most intimate secrets. For he is able to discern in others a scarcely articulated need, the whole of their capacity to desire what is good. Thus he hastens to satisfy this desire and gives himself entirely to doing so. But he also discerns in others their impurities, even those they hide most skilfully. Then his compassion becomes purifying through the gentle strength of his own purity, and through the suffering caused him by the evil intentions of others or their perverse desires. This suffering remains with him always.

In each of these situations he knows when it is opportune to speak, and what needs to be said; he also knows when to keep silence and what ought to be done. One might consider this subtle discernment on the part of the saints as a sort of 'pastoral diplomacy', a further expression of their distinction and nobility of character.

The saint always radiates a spirit of generosity, of forbearance, of attention and willingness to share, without any thought for himself. His warmth gives warmth to others and makes them feel they are regaining their strength, and lets them experience the joy of not being alone. The saint is like an innocent lamb, always ready to be sacrificed and to take to himself the suffering of others, but he is also an unshakeable wall against which all can lean for support. In sharing thus the lot of others the saint sometimes shows great discretion, while at other times he expresses himself without reserve. It is hardly necessary to speak of the total absence of self-interest in his relationships.

Moreover, no one is humbler than the saint, more free from all that is artificial, further from any kind of boasting, more 'natural' in his behaviour, because he accepts and understands everything that is truly human, all those lowly and sometimes ridiculous aspects of our humanity, which is great only when it is not boasting of its greatness. Thus the saint immediately creates an atmosphere of friendliness, of kinship and indeed of intimacy between himself and others. In this way he humanizes his relationships and leaves on them a mark of genuineness, because he himself has become profoundly human and genuine. He speaks kindly and avoids naming the weaknesses of others with brutal franknesss; but at the same time he creates the conditions for a direct, candid and open relationship between himself and others. He urges them to confess their weaknesses and sins sincerely, and fortifies them in their struggle to overcome them.

St Maximus the Confessor says that the saints have attained to a pure simplicity, because they have overcome in themselves all duality and pretence. They have passed beyond the struggle between soul and body, between good intentions and works performed, between deceitful appearances and hidden thoughts, between what they pretend to be and what they actually are. They have become simple because they have given themselves entirely to God. That is why they are able also to give themselves entirely to men in their relationships with them. If at times they choose not to name weaknesses outright, they do so in order not to discourage people, and also because in themselves discretion, delicacy, gratitude, simplicity and sincerity are continually growing.

The saints always give encouragement. Sometimes they do it by reducing the exaggerated proportions in which men tend to see their own weaknesses, sins and passions. They free them from feelings of despair or of utter powerlessness. But sometimes also they subdue the pride of others with a light humour. They smile, but do not laugh loudly or sarcastically. At other times, faced with acts that are immoral or with blameworthy passions, they disclose the full seriousness of these things, but without inspiring fear. They ascribe an infinite value to the humblest of men, because the Son of God himself, in becoming incarnate, has given this infinite value to every man. They see Christ in all men, as some of the Fathers have expressed it in their sayings. But at the same time they humble the pride of others by themselves presenting an example of humility. Thus they constantly re-establish the natural equality between men.

Because of his humility the saint is scarcely noticed, but he is always there when anyone has need of support, consolation or encouragement. He stands by the one whom everyone else abandons. With him no difficulty is insurmountable, no obstacle invincible, when it is a matter of drawing someone out of a situation of despair. At such times he shows an astonishing strength and skill, together with unshakeable calm and confidence, because he believes firmly in the help of God, seeking it with urgent prayer.

He is the most humble and human of men, but at the same time an unconventional and surprising figure. He gives others the feeling that they have discovered in him, and therefore in themselves because of him, the nature of true humanity.

This humanity has been so overlaid by artificiality, by the desire to *appear* rather than to *be*, that when it reveals its true self it causes astonishment, as if it were something unnatural. The saint is the most courteous of men, yet at the same time, quite unintentionally he compels recognition. He is the one who attracts most attention and inspires most respect. He becomes the intimate friend of each one, the person who best understands you and puts you at your ease, and at the same time stirs you up by making you aware of how much you fall short and of the sins you avoid looking at. He overwhelms you by the simple grandeur of his purity and by the warmth of his goodness and consideration; he makes you ashamed of having such low standards, of having disfigured human nature in yourself, of being impure, artificial, full of duplicity and meanness. All this is highlighted by the comparison which you involuntarily make between yourself and him.

The saint does not exercise any earthly power; he does not issue his orders with severity. So no critical thoughts of him rise up in you, and you feel no resentment towards him. For he makes the person of Christ real for you in his gentleness and strength. Thus you do not try to hide from him or avoid his eye; or it may indeed happen that you do seek to avoid him, more than you would someone who imposed strict commands on you. For you sense in him an irreducible firmness, the total identification of his being with goodness, although again, this firmness of his in his convictions, his life, in the opinions and advice he gives, is a firmness which is neither tense nor rigid.

That is why, by their wholly paradoxical character, the opinions and counsels he enjoins upon you so gently acquire a greater authority for you than any earthly precept; and so you would make any effort, undergo any sacrifice in order to carry them out. For the tenderness of the saint is at the same time firmness and goodness. Both come from the divine radiance, and show forth the character of the divine goodness which, with an absolute authority, declares itself in gentleness. In the same way, the counsel of a saint comes to you as a liberation. It delivers you from the disfigurement and powerlessness of your state and from a supreme lack of confidence. You experience what the saint has said to you as a strength, and as a sure light on the way of salvation in which you must walk if you are to save yourself from acquiescing in the loss of your own soul. What you feel coming to you from the saint is not only strength and light, but also the goodness that flows from the supreme source of goodness. You shrink from the gaze of the saint penetrating the depths of your soul, just as you are afraid that he will discover there some truth discreditable to you, but at the same time you await the discovery as if it were that of a doctor who is both unquestionably competent and a steadfast friend. He will give you, as you well know, the diagnosis and the effective remedy for an illness which you vaguely sense to be a mortal one.

In the kindness, gentleness and humility of the saint you perceive a power that no earthly power can turn aside to make him fall from his purity of heart, from his love for God and men, from the determination to give himself totally to God and to the service of men, to help them attain salvation.

Anyone who approaches a saint discovers in him a supreme goodness and purity veiled in a humility which makes him still more attractive. It requires some effort to discover the heroic quality of his renunciations, of his asceticism and of his love for men; but his greatness makes itself felt in the kindness, the simplicity, humility and purity which emanate from him. In him exalted goodness and neighbourliness coincide. He exemplifies greatness in *kenosis*, or humility. The person of a saint radiates a calm and a peace which nothing can disturb. But this calm and peace are won and maintained by hard struggle. At the same time the saint shares in the griefs of others even to tears. He is rooted in the stability of the love and suffering of God incarnate, for this love shines forth from the God who was himself made man and who has suffered for men. The saint rests in the eternity of the power and goodness of God which, in Christ, as St Maximus the Confessor tells us, have become available for men; for like Melchisedek, his whole being bears witness to the presence of God. But his stability in the eternal love of God and of men does not exclude him from sharing in the sorrows of men or in their aspirations to goodness, just as Christ does not cease to be a perpetual sacrifice for them, just as the angels never cease to offer their ministry. For stability in suffering and succouring love, this too is eternity, a living eternity. This is the 'rest', the stability, the sabbath into which the saints have entered (Heb. 3:18-4:11), those who have left the Egypt of the passions. It is not the sabbath of an insensible Nirvana; for by resting in the eternity of unshakeable love, the love of God for men, the saint has power to draw others towards eternity and help them to overcome their suffering with courage, and not to give way to despair. Thus he is the forerunner and sustainer of humankind on the road which leads to the perfect fulfilment of the Last Day.

The saint has triumphed over time while living intensely within time. He has thus come to bear the closest resemblance to Christ, who is at once in the heavenly places, and always with us, bringing mighty things to pass. He bears Christ within himself with the invincible power to his love, for the salvation of men.

The saint shows us a human being purified from the dross of all that is less than human. In him we see a disfigured and brutalised humanity set to rights; a humanity whose restored transparency reveals the limitless goodness, the boundless power and compassion of its prototype—God incarnate. It is the image of the living and personal absolute Being who became man that is re-established in the person of the saint. By being so truly human, he has reached a dizzy height of perfection in God, while remaining completely at home with men. The saint is one who is engaged in ceaseless, free dialogue with God and with men. His transparency reveals the dawn of the divine eternal light in which human nature is to reach its fulfilment. He is the complete reflection of the humanity of Christ.

II

PURE PRAYER, OR PRAYER OF THE HEART, AND OBSTACLES IN THE WAY

PART OF WHAT I am going to say is what I have learned from a Romanian monk. He himself practises this prayer of the heart which is founded largely on the tradition of the Fathers of the East. In part also these are some reflections on that teaching.

Pure prayer is concerned with the reuniting of the mind *(nous)* and the heart. Neither mind nor heart can be allowed to remain alone. Prayer that comes only from the mind is cold; prayer that comes only from the heart is sentimental and is ignorant of all that God has given us, is giving us now and will give us in Christ. It is prayer without horizon or perspective, prayer in which we do not know what to thank God for, what to praise him for, what to ask him for. The man who prays in this way has the feeling of being lost in an impersonal infinity. Such a feeling knows nothing of encounter with a personal God. And thus it is not prayer .

We must also be quite clear that this meeting between mind and heart is not brought about by the ascent of the heart into the mind, but by the descent of the mind into the heart. In other words, it is not in the mind that the heart finds its rest; but it is in the heart (or rather where the depths of the heart meet the depths of God) that the mind finds the rest for which it is searching.

Certainly the Fathers speak also of an opening of the mind to the infinity of God, but it seems to be in the heart that this opening of the mind takes place. By its search for God the mind itself enters into the reality of the depth of the heart and knows it as depth set apart for God, the true Infinity. Deep calls to deep (Psalm 42:9). The infinity of God cannot be experienced apart from his love for us. This love of God for us calls to our love, and it is with the heart, the organ of love within us, that we experience his love. But we are speaking here of a heart that knows, thanks to the mind which has entered it, that this infinity is the infinity of a God who is personal, and that God enters into intimate relationship with us through Christ. That is why it is the mind which comes to rest in the heart. In the heart it finds the infinity of God. It is not the heart that comes to rest in the mind, for that would mean that the feeling of the infinity of God had become a theory, chilled by thought. It is not feeling that must be chilled by thought, but thought which must warm itself in the feeling of the heart in real contact with the infinity of God, and thus give this feeling a definite content.

Strictly speaking, when the mind has descended into the heart we no longer encounter God through ideas, but through that awareness of his presence which enables us to submit our thoughts to the test of reality. Here the sense of an unattained reality which the mind experiences is resolved in the immediate presence of God. The idea of God, or our ideas about him, are fulfilled and penetrated, pierced through by *awareness of the living reality of God.* The reality takes the place of the idea and at the same time verifies it; the idea no longer comes between us and God. Thus the heart is for the mind a sort of sensory organ in relation to God, just as the bodily senses are the apparatus which enable us to perceive and feel the realities with which the body enters into relation.

There are however obstacles that can hinder the mind when it wants to enter the heart, to penetrate beyond ideas into experience of the reality of God, and at the same time to verify the content of its ideas. These obstacles come partly from physical sensations or from the imaginations which reflect them and to which they give rise. In part also they come from the difficulty which the mind itself has in passing beyond the ideas which are quite natural to it, but these obstacles are only meant to supply the intellect with provisional intimations of the unfelt reality of God, not to imprison it.

The feelings or imaginings which tend to prevent the mind from entering into the heart and so attaining to pure prayer, or prayer of the heart, are either those which are the result of sin, or an attraction towards sin, or those which make us think we are being drawn towards good actions or a real meeting with God himself, but which in fact do not lead to God. That is why the Fathers warn monks even against images that seem to be good. They exhort them not to rely on any kind of imagination or impression. Moreover the Fathers consider thought, even theological thought to be a no less dangerous obstacle to the mind's entry into the heart. They must be watchful not to rest in theological thinking, or to slip into it, when they are moved to prayer or while they are praying. Thinking about God interrupts direct encounter with him. By theological thinking a man becomes shut in on himself.

The Fathers speak of prayer as consisting of a single thought (*monologistos euche*). Strictly speaking it is not even a thought, but rather an awareness of being totally absorbed in the reality of God. One can, nevertheless, call this conscious experience 'thought', because it is not simply a state of confused feeling or the sensation of being lost in the ocean of inarticulate reality, but it is awareness of encounter with the personal infinity of God who loves us. It is the mind's confirmation of the reality. I do not lose myself in this infinity, because it is the infinity of a personal God and of his love to which I respond with my love. For the heart is truly the place where one experiences the love of the other, and where one responds to the other. I do not lose myself, because it is the infinity of a personal God whose love is my delight; I depend on his love as I depend on his mercy, for face to face with him I still feel infinitely small, and a sinner.

This encounter in love, and at the same time this sense of the infinite difference between God and myself, this need I feel for the mercy of God, all this is expressed in the Jesus Prayer. The heart is the source of feeling and therefore of love; and love means meeting the other. And because love is impelled by a movement of infinite desire it can only be fully satisfied in encounter with God, the Infinite.

But the heart is also the source of sorrow and the place where sorrow is felt. Before the face of God the heart knows sorrow for sin and for the offence caused by sin. In his heart man weeps and asks for forgiveness. Tears well up from the heart, tears of penitence, but also tears of joy. There man lets go of his settled habits of mind. If, however, the heart sinks to a lower level, it becomes the place of the passions, that is, of an infinite attachment to the world and to oneself—to persons and things that are finite. So just as the heart can radiate infinite love it can also radiate infinite hatred when it meets with an obstacle to those sinful attachments. Good thoughts and good words come from the heart, but also thoughts of greed, hatred and murder. Even evil thoughts and words receive some quality of infinity from the heart, although they have to do with things that are finite. But this infinite attachment to finite things cannot satisfy the truly infinite thirst of the heart. Only the meeting of the heart with God can satisfy that thirst. And therefore the heart must be freed from the passions, from attachment to finite things, by its capacity for the infinite.

In the encounter with God the infinite is perceived as limitless joy and limitless light. In expressing this in words man can only hint at the joy which is beyond all limitation. The words of the Jesus Prayer express, albeit feebly, this sense of joy, of gratitude, of love and of infinite humility. But formulating words is not what really matters. What matters *is* the joy, the gratitude, the love and the humility, even the infinite sorrow caused by sin. Then the words are no longer an object of reflection for the one who utters them. They no longer come between man and God but in them man addresses God in God's own presence. The presence of God supplies whatever is lacking.

The words are now both uttered and transcended in the same moment. Thus they do not deceive us with a semblance of independent reality, but they are the expression of immediate contact with the reality of God. Our attention is not directed to the words but to God, to whom they are addressed as in a dialogue. But we can also live in this dialogue without any words.

That is why the monk to whom I referred earlier said that at an advanced stage of prayer one can even give up the Jesus Prayer. Only its content need be retained. One turns to God and one's very being expresses the praise of God, the sense of wonder before him, of gratitude and humility. This state of profound feeling is more adequately expressed by the whole being than by words for what is being expressed is beyond words. It is pure prayer, prayer of the whole being, in which the feelings have moved out beyond all things, all thoughts, beyond the very self, to the encounter with God. This exodus of the feelings is lived out in the heart in a state of intense prayer. In the heart the whole being is impelled towards God in love, with feelings of a love which is boundless.

III

HOLINESS: GOD SHINING THROUGH THE CONSCIOUSNESS OF MAN

IN THE SAINT God reveals himself as transcendent, as different from the world. Holiness is the luminous and active mystery of God present in all his transcendence, a mystery which enlightens and transforms. Holiness cannot therefore be the attribute of some impersonal reality belonging to the natural order: what is impersonal lacks the depths of mystery. Holiness belongs to the order of mystery; that is why it can only be the attribute of God himself in his nature as transcendent person. God, the unfathomably personal, imparts himself in his transcendence. Hence the paradoxical nature of holiness: it is at one and the same time transcendence and self-disclosure, or communication.

Since holiness is an attribute of the transcendent and therefore mysterious person of God we are seized with trembling and overwhelmed with shame in its presence; for it is the manifestation of a conscience* superior to our own, one which makes us see our wickedness. Holiness is the radiance shining from a transcendent person whose object in revealing himself is to raise us up to him. We feel impelled to leave our sinful state so as to be able to remain in his presence, while at the same time this radiance enlightens our own conscience, making it more sensitive to sin. It is as if the holiness of God invaded the human conscience with supreme transcendent urgency, kindling in us the desire for purification and a longing for what is greater than ourselves. This new birth of humility and desire for purification constitute true self-knowledge. In the presence of holiness our conscience develops an extreme sensitivity; this can come about only because our conscience has received the revelation of one that is superior. St Symeon the New Theologian says: 'When the soul has

**Translators' Note*: The French word *conscience*, used throughout the text has the double meaning of the English words 'conscience' and 'consciousness'; wherever either of these words is used in this translation, both meanings are to be understood.

received this imprint, when through the grace of the Holy Spirit its thought has been immersed in the depths of humility in Christ our God, it ceases from then on to attend to the world or to those who are of the world and turns its whole attention to itself; and when, through perseverance, this kind of meditation has become habitual to it, the soul no longer sees anything but itself in its insignificance and utter abasement, and is convinced that there is no soul in all the world as unworthy as itself'.

Through the grace of divine light, the intuition of personal unworthiness and an acute sensitivity of conscience are paradoxically united before the glory of God, the glory of a supreme conscience which awakens conscience in us. Only a superior conscience can awaken another conscience; only the light of God can raise a man's consciousness to its highest point, while at the same time giving him a clear perception of his insignificance. What is impersonal does not arouse shame, does not sharpen conscience. It is the luminous fire of a God who *is* conscience that burns us when his holiness impinges on us in the insistence that we should be holy as he is holy. Penetrated by the holiness of God as supreme conscience, man becomes a burning bush; or again, in the presence of a holy man he feels that he is standing before a burning bush. The shame, the awe, experienced in the presence of holiness exceeds any that can arise in response to human beings; it is of another order, because the divine reality of the supreme conscience made visible to us in the conscience of a saint shows us ourselves exactly as we are, and reveals itself as supremely urgent, judging our sinful condition. And yet, at the same time, holiness attracts us. In *The Ecclesiastical Hierarchy* Dionysius the Areopagite identifies the holiness of God with his perfect purity, and his sanctifying action with his purifying action.

The perfect purity of God then evokes not only fear but also joy, for this exposure of our inmost being, as well as showing up our sin, has shown also what is good in us; it has awakened in us the desire to be cleansed from sin in order to be pleasing to the consciousness of God. We are glad because God the Holy One has made it possible for us to become pure, to leave our wickedness behind; we can exchange our torpor for a vital existence, drawn from the very source of all existence, the person of God in his burning charity. We are glad because God the Holy One has not utterly rejected us, but has awakened in us the desire to purify ourselves. We are glad because we have been relieved of a burden we had been carrying unawares and an obstacle to fullness of life has been taken away. We are glad because we are no longer hypocritically acting a part which was bringing us to the point where we no longer recognized ourselves or had the courage to be ourselves, for fear that the wickedness of our hearts would be laid bare.

Thus we find our inmost being set free to live a new life in real communication with others. Those who feel themselves forgiven by God and freed from the state of sin have a certain boldness (*parresia*) before God and before others. They are open and straightforward and enjoy great freedom in their relationships. There is nothing presumptuous in this, just the innocent candour of a child who is unaware of any taint of sin. It is a candour imbued with profound trust in God and in others; a man comes out of himself and attaches himself to God and to other people; he acts in such a way that God and other people open their doors to him. The saint is far from the uncertainty that shuts a man in on himself. The innocent daring of purity and trust is the means of his union with others. Thus the saint attains *rest* in God and in other men, just as God and others, in their turn, find their *rest* in him (cf. Hebrews 3:18). 'For you are Holy, O our God, and in the saints you take your rest', sings the Eastern Church. That God does rest in his saints is a fact of which they always remain vividly aware. It means also that God takes pleasure in the saints, just as the saints feel at ease when they rest in God. Human consciousness can feel at ease only in another consciousness, embraced by the loving awareness of another person. This is the supreme mutual indwelling, the coinherence of the consciousness of two people.

In order to become the resting-place of God, or to find its own resting-place in God, the spirit of man must itself be capable of assimilating a consciousness of infinite depth and radiance. God must find in it scope for extending his light infinitely, a capacity for limitless increase in depth. Man must be capable of continually renewing and deepening his conscious experience of God; and God in his turn delights in this perpetual renewal of joy in the man in whom he rests. Man must always be responding afresh to the experience of God; for only if he does can God himself have the joy of continually resting in man. The man in whom God rests and who rests in God must reflect the infinity of the conscious light of God; the infinity of God must become proper to man, by grace. That is what is meant by the divinization of man in God and the humanization of God in man. It is the union of God and man in the Holy Spirit, the Spirit of light: the illuminating Spirit of God becomes the Spirit who illuminates man by grace. The divine consciousness and the human consciousness become transparent to each other, coinherent. By affirming that this mutual penetration without confusion occurs between God and man, Christianity has revealed the unfathomable and indefinable mystery of the human person and his consciousness.

It has been said that Christianity has eliminated the sacred from the world and from human life. In fact the reverse is true. Christianity has revealed the aptitude of every man for holiness, and the aptitude of the whole world for reflecting that holiness. It has done this by revealing man's capacity to bear consciously within him the infinity of God and to make unlimited progress into God, the infinity of consciousness; the Son of God being himself infinite light and consciousness, has taken human nature upon himself. Human nature has thus become the vehicle for the manifestation of the infinite light, or the infinitely profound consciousness, of the divine hypostasis; it has become able to rejoice in it and to reflect it. The divine hypostasis in its infinite consciousness has entered into the depths of the life of human nature for ever, without itself suffering any limitation; our natural human life moves eternally in the boundless ocean of the consciousness of the divine hypostasis, without itself being dissolved. There is a capacity for infinite divine consciousness in all that is human, in the human patterns of thought, of feeling, of joy, of love, of communion, which nevertheless remain human patterns.

The Fathers saw sanctity as an ever increasing likeness of man to God, brought about by the purification of the passions, and by growth in the virtues which culminate in boundless love. This implies a deepening of the human conscience, illuminated by the light of the consciousness of God. According to the Fathers the virtues are the attributes of God in their human expression, that is, they are the ever-deepening reflection of his light, his consciousness, in the consciousness of man. Through the virtues God first of all becomes man in man, and then he causes man to become God. This means that through the virtues human consciousness never ceases to expand. The virtues are the wings on which man soars ever higher into the light of God, while his conscience descends ever deeper. But he is never dissolved in God. He is able, and feels the need, to fly to an ever greater height, constantly to assimilate more of the good things of God, to let his consciousness expand—for all being culminates eternally in God, the source of all good, the infinite source of all consciousness or light.

Thus the likeness of man to God, in which holiness consists, is precisely this continuous movement of man into God, this ever more intense mutual interpenetration, ever more brilliant enlightenment of human conscience by the infinitely luminous consciousness of God. Holiness is that transparency whereby the spirit of man, filled completely with the light of the Holy Spirit, is reflected through his body and radiates around him. This radiance of the divine consciousness extends even to his face and to his actions.

In this transparency to God, at once ethereal and concentrated, man realizes his true nature, which, on the spiritual plane, consists in self-communication. Communication means exchange between two or more conscious beings. The greater the transparency, the greater the communication. When man does not communicate sincerely, when he loses his transparency, he is hiding and starving his true nature made in the image of God, and his capacity to be responsible for his brothers.

My face reveals the light in which my conscience shows me the face of my fellow-man for whom I feel responsible. How much more do the faces of the saints reveal the light in which their conscience shows them the face of God before whom they are responsible, and the faces of other men for whom they feel responsible before God. This intensifies the radiance in the face of a holy man; his own light and the light of those whom he bears on his heart is joined with the light that comes to them all from God. It is the light of goodness, and goodness always has a tripersonal character. It is the goodness of a man, but in the end it it is the goodness of God, for all goodness comes from him; and it is goodness directed towards another. Goodness cannot exist without a recipient, and the one who receives this goodness also has a part to play in making it possible for the other to become good. Light must have a field in which to project itself. That is why the chief work of the saints is their prayer for the salvation of men.

IV

PRAYER AND FREEDOM

PRAYER sets man free, releasing him from servitude both to external nature and to himself. Prayer keeps the soul open to God as Person. The man who does not pray remains a slave, enclosed in the complex mechanisms of the natural world and of the movements of his own passions, by which he is dominated even more than by the world outside.

Prayer assures freedom to man in relation to the complex mechanisms of the external world, which are produced by the interaction of the laws of nature. By praying man affirms his conviction that these mechanisms are merely contingent, having their origin in the free intervention of the sovereign Person who created them. This conviction is supported by the fact that even human persons have the freedom to manipulate certain mechanisms of the laws of nature and direct them towards goals of their own choice. My mind has the power to make my body execute the movements I have chosen; through these movements and through the tools which extend their action, my mind has power over things and over the forces of nature. All men are alike in possessing this power. If I make requests to other men, if I 'pray' to them, I can get them to intervene in the mechanism of natural laws in ways useful to myself. Thus by means of natural objects and forces in the natural order men can develop a free dialogue among themselves. Each man asserts his own freedom when he acts within the natural order, and he affirms the freedom of other men when he makes requests to them.

May we not therefore also believe in the possibility of intervention by the sovereign Person who created nature and its laws? If nature manifests a general state of contingency in relation to the human mind, this proves that it has been created as a field of contingency open to the intervention of free beings, the field of a free dialogue between men. It has therefore been created in the service of freedom, by the One who is himself free. Why then should not this creative Freedom continue to intervene in the contingent mechanisms of nature, and to do so more effectively than is possible for human freedom? The world has no meaning except as a sphere for dialogue between God and men. Men respond to the deeds of God in the world with deeds of their own. But in their prayer they ask God to intervene. Their prayer is an affirmation of awareness that the freedom of God does intervene in the world for their good. In prayer they affirm their conviction of being something more than cogs in the wheels of nature. In prayer they recognize themselves as being objects of God's special concern.

It might be objected that man can intervene in nature because his mind is so closely interwoven with his physical make-up (and therefore with his immediate surroundings) that his movements inevitably have repercussions on those of nature. But why should we not also allow that there is a connection between God and the world so close as to make them inseparable; that the world is rooted in God, and that the movements of God's will, unconditioned as they are, always leave their imprint on the conditioned world? And so, just as the link between the human spirit and material nature is a great and impenetrable mystery, the link between God and the world is a mystery even greater and more impenetrable. We shall in any case never find pure matter as a separate substance either in the human body or in any of the things accessible to man through his senses. Far less shall we ever find the material substance of the whole world utterly destitute of the divine spirit. If we ever did, that would imply a world which, as a self-enclosed mechanism, entirely governed by scientific laws, would be ultimately without meaning. Against this the prayer of man affirms and actualizes the dialogue in which man and God engage freely, in this world and beyond it.

But prayer also asserts and actualizes man's liberation from his passions and from himself. The passions are chains binding man to external nature, making him its slave. If science tells him in theory that he is the slave of nature, his passions make him its slave in practical and moral terms. They enslave him to a nature that is debased, that has in him run wild. This again shows that we can never find nature in its pure essence. The passions are a mingling of spirit and nature—but of an enfeebled spirit which has perverted nature, and a nature which, thus perverted, dominates the spirit.

Prayer helps us to escape from the passions and it presupposes liberation from them. Again it might be objected that the man who does not pray can still master his passions by exercising his freedom, and in this way he too can rise above the unfree inclinations of his lower nature. But if man recognizes nothing beyond his own liberty, he still remains enslaved to a passion, namely to his pride, which is no less a passion than any of the others. He himself chooses the criterion of his actions. And where does he think this will lead him if he does not acknowledge God? In the last analysis he will remain a prisoner in the realm of blind nature, and be dissolved by death.

Prayer then is that which raises a man above himself. It is only by escaping from himself, from what is thought to be his freedom of choice, that man escapes from nature and from death. It is only when he is set free from himself that man becomes free in the true sense of the word, in the sense, that is, of not being dominated by any of the passions. Evagrius Ponticus says: 'The state of prayer can be aptly described as a habitual state of imperturbable calm (*apatheia*). It snatches to the heights of intelligible reality the spirit which loves wisdom and which is truly spiritualized by the most intense love.' (*Chapters on Prayer*, Cistercian Studies Series No. 4. ch.52, p. 63.)

In prayer man attains freedom in respect to nature, because he finds himself in direct relationship with God, who, as sovereign Person, is above nature and above all passion. 'Prayer is a continual intercourse of the spirit with God. What state of soul then is required that the spirit might thus strain after its Master without wavering, living constantly with him without intermediary?' (Evagrius Ponticus, op. cit. ch. 3, p. 56.)

Only a relationship of pure love with another person can set us free from the world outside and from ourselves. But only God can give us and inspire in us such a love towards every other person. In our relationship with God we obtain true and lasting freedom from ourselves, for he draws us so powerfully by the infinite riches of his Person and the generosity of his love that we forget ourselves in him. Consequently our relationship with God endows us with total freedom with regard to nature and to ourselves, and further, makes us capable of expressing this freedom in our relationships with human persons.

It is because prayer is able to do this for us that we recognize it as the highest activity of the spirit, for our spirit tends of its very nature and has the intrinsic power, to rise and to lift us above ourselves, enabling us to enter into and remain in a relationship of pure love with another person. This tendency and this power come from the spirit's living relationship with the supreme Person. True liberty is affirmed and maintained in a relationship of pure love with another person, and ultimately with the sovereign Person. For the sovereign Person will never be dominated by any kind of force in the natural order, and will therefore not be tempted to dominate in order to avoid being dominated himself. In our relationship with God we are perfectly free, because God, dominated by nothing himself, does not seek to dominate. Only in the relationship between authentically free beings is the freedom of each person assured; neither is dominated, neither wishes to dominate.

We can never secure our own freedom by dominating others. There is no true freedom in isolation; if a man entrenches himself in isolation, there he remains, for it is impossible for any one to free himself from himself. Wanting to be lord over himself, man then finds that he is subject to himself; similarly, in his relationship with nature, wanting to lord it over the natural world he becomes its slave. Certainly man must be over nature, but that is a very different thing from the passionate desire to dominate it; man is lord of nature indeed only when he is free in relation to it.

Only another authentically free being, one, that is, who is free from all passion and who has therefore no desire to dominate, will affirm and uphold my freedom. Only in the relationship with the sovereign Person whose freedom cannot be threatened is my own freedom guaranteed.

This does not mean that the relationship between free beings is something exterior, a relationship which leaves each one separate in his own freedom. On the contrary, each becomes a kind of support for the freedom of the other. True freedom makes the freedom of the other a reality. In my own freedom I sense the freedom of the person with whom I share a relationship. His freedom is not such that he has no interest in me, neither is it such that he wants to dominate me; it is a freedom which acts upon me through love, through respect for my freedom and for the person I am.

When I turn to someone seeking for attention, or love, they are given to me because I want them, they are called forth by my freedom. If that person gives me his love and attention without wishing to dominate me he sets me free from myself. For, not seeking to defend my freedom, I forget myself. I live freely on the gift of his love, on his freedom from any desire to dominate me. Thus the true liberty of another person supports mine. Only in the ambience of another person's freedom does my freedom become a reality. Only another person's freedom can nourish and affirm mine. But it is only in the ambience of the uncreated Freedom that all the created freedoms can be affirmed. These sustain each other by love, mutually sought and given.

In my relation to God, of course, my prayer is not reciprocated: God does not pray to man, man prays to God. There is, however, mutual giving. Man realizes his freedom not only by receiving it from God through prayer but also by giving himself to God. Only so does man gain freedom from himself. If he tries to hold on to the existence he has received from God in love, he loses his freedom; wanting to be arbiter of his own existence he becomes its slave. If he is to be free from himself, he must be willing to receive life always as the gift of God. He must renounce himself and give himself to God, from whom he receives all that he has. He can only be free if he lives for God and in God. He cannot mount guard over his freedom against the very One who gives it to him, but has to receive it continually from God in prayer. As soon as man seeks to dominate what he has, he becomes the slave of passion, and therefore of himself.

We have to give ourselves to another authentically free being in order to receive the gift of freedom, and the only freedom which is of its nature inexhaustible is that of the supreme Person.

Prayer is the reverse of the will to dominate. That is why it guarantees the freedom of man; it affirms another Freedom, and that Freedom assures freedom to the one who prays. True prayer is prayer addressed to God; it is the encounter with Freeom itself, boundless Freedom which nothing can threaten and which therefore presents no threat. This Freedom desires to affirm and uphold the freedom of every person who is content to be thus affirmed without affirming himself.

As the expression of free relationship with God, that is, as a manifestation of the Holy Spirit, prayer already has within it the power of the Spirit of God, strengthening the spirit of man and making his relationship with God a reality. 'Likewise the Spirit helps us in our weakness; for we do not know how to pray as we ought, but the Spirit himself intercedes for us with sighs too deep for words' (Rom. 8:26). The Spirit creates so close a relationship between ourselves and God that we feel we are the sons of God, and our union with God in prayer is so perfect and complete that we can no longer tell where our work ends and God's work begins. God's action becomes our own and thus we are saved not by our own righteousness but by the righteousness of God. In the Spirit we forget ourselves so thoroughly, we leave ourselves behind so completely that we can no longer distinguish our action from the action of the Spirit of God. The liberty of the Spirit of God has become our own liberty and our weakness has become the weakness of God. It is no longer we who pray and thereby affirm our liberty, but the Spirit of God. It is in the weakness of prayer that the strength of God's freedom, which has become our freedom, is affirmed. It is in our going beyond ourselves that God's going beyond himself is revealed to us through the Spirit. This ultimate union, which is lived out in a paradoxical way, also expresses, one might say, our state as sons by divine adoption. In prayer we give ourselves completely to God and God gives himself completely to us, as the Father to his children. And we have in us the freedom of the sons of God. We do not feel that we are dominated by God like slaves, but that we are free, heirs of his freedom, born of his freedom and living in freedom.

V

FORGIVENESS AND THE RENEWAL OF THE CHURCH

OUR LORD has indissolubly linked the forgiveness of sins with the forgiveness we owe to those who have wronged us (the Lord's Prayer, Matt. 6:12, and the Parable of the Two Debtors, Matt. 18:21-35).

In most cases, the sins for which we ask God to forgive us are in fact wrongs we have done to other men. Consequently we should ask forgiveness for these sins not only of God but also of those whom they have injured. Unless we do, God will not forgive us (Matt. 5: 23-26). Behind the people we have wronged there is always God; when it is God we have sinned against, there are always other people involved. If we despise God we impair the capacity for goodness in other men by setting them a bad example. A man who is insensitive in his behaviour towards God will be no less insensitive in his behaviour towards others and will help, moreover, to blunt their sensitivity towards God.

God forgives us, then, for the sins we have committed against him only on condition that we ask forgiveness of our fellow-men. But if we need the forgiveness of others before we can receive that of God, they too need our forgiveness in order to receive his. And so, to obtain God's forgivensss we need to forgive those who have wronged us, and at the same time to ask pardon of those whom we ourselves have wronged. Both things are very difficult for us to do. We find it easier to ask God to forgive us, because we stand in a certain sense in awe of his majesty, and it is easy for us, as believers, to acknowledge in theory our dependence on him. On the other hand it is very difficult, even when we believe in God, not to despise men who do not impress us with any visible marks of greatness.

Again, of the two obligations we have, to forgive others and to ask for their forgiveness, it is the latter that we find harder. When other people ask us to forgive them, they seem to be putting themselves in a position of inferiority, and our heart is touched through this appeal to our pride. To ask pardon for ourselves implies coming down from our pedestal of apparent superiority; it implies that we recognize our dependence on others.

It is always the same pride that lurks behind our refusal to forgive and behind the effort it costs us to ask for forgiveness. When we forgive we have not necessarily renounced all our pride; whereas if we go further, if we actually ask for forgiveness, we have done away with it to the last shred. For it is only then that we are genuinely moved by a pure impulse of the heart, without any ambiguity.

The refusal to grant forgiveness or to ask for it keeps our soul in a state of rigidity. If we retain the memory of a wrong done to us, it lodges in us as an impurity; it festers in us continually and its loathsome smell pervades our whole being. The false lights or shadows of this poisonous matter obstruct our vision and we cannot look at the other with purity. In this situation we cannot love the other, neither can the other love us.

Only sincere forgiveness can expel this intruder from our soul and cast out the beam from our eye. Only so can we receive God's loving forgiveness. Abba Isaiah said: 'Bear no ill-will towards another man, that your labours may not be in vain; purify your heart towards all men, that you may see in yourself the peace of God. For just as, if a man is stung by a scorpion, its venom spreads through his whole body until it reaches his heart, so it is when there is malice in our heart towards our neighbour; its venom wounds the soul and imperils it in consequence of this evil. Thus, the man who is anxious not to lose the fruit of his labours at once shakes off this scorpion of malice and ill-will.'

In the same way, the evil we have done to another troubles our soul. We feel uneasy; we cannot look at the other person directly, with unclouded eyes. Whenever we meet him we feel awkward, for we suspect him of brooding over the memory of the wrong we have done him. My pride will not allow me to purify my relations with him. Only a request on my part for his forgiveness can bring us into a relationship that is open, candid and free. If I persist in my proud refusal to ask for it, I cannot face God openly and stand before him in compunction of heart. Behind this request for forgiveness there must be a sincere and lively sense of penitence. Penitence lends a permanent expression of sadness to the eyes, but the same eyes that are filled with this sadness still keep their candid and unclouded gaze. It is thus, with simple and sincere penitence, that I must come before God to ask his forgiveness, having first asked forgiveness of my fellow-men.

My sins before God are innumerable and there is no end to them. All that I have comes to me from God and I should freely give it all back to him and to others. I should be continually praising him for his goodness, in word and deed; but I fail to do so. And for that reason I need perpetually to renew my penitence, my prayer for his forgiveness and mercy. That is why the Eastern monk implores the mercy of God in prayer without ceasing. Thus, at the moment of his death, we see St Antony the Great asking for more time for repentance. And since the sins we commit against God are also sins against our fellow-men, and vice versa, so there is no end to our sinning against others, and so too, we must continually be asking their forgiveness.

In any case, I can hardly claim that in my relationships with others my own conduct has at all times been beyond reproach, or that I have done all the good I could and should have done for all the people I have met. So when someone reproaches me with a negative attitude of which I was not even aware, I ought to accept his reproach and acknowledge that I am to blame. At the very least I am at fault in giving the impression of having this negative attitude of which I am accused. Abba Isaiah said: 'If your brother answers you impatiently, with a sharp word, bear it with joy, and if you examine your thoughts according to the judgement of God, you will find that you have sinned.' I can never be quite certain that I have had no part in creating the unavoidable frictions which constantly arise among men and which also affect me. I can hardly make the assertion that in relation to others everything in my own conduct, thoughts and words is good; that I have been so generous in my attention to others that they cannot possibly have felt I was indifferent to them. We are all guilty of offences against all.

We must therefore be penitent for our treatment of our fellow-men. That is why we always commend ourselves to the celebrant of the Liturgy, asking that our name be mentioned in the Preparation, and why we ask everyone we meet to pray for us. And we too have the obligation to remember in our prayers, as far as possible, all whom we know, and in general to make remembrance of all men. Our forgiveness of others is implicit in our prayer for them, and our request for their prayers implies that we seek forgiveness.

We pray for the dead whom we have known, and in praying for them we actually forgive them, and at the same time seek to ensure that after our own death we shall have the prayers of those who live on and the prayers of the Church as a whole. In this way we ask them to forgive us after our death, not just once, but to go on forgiving us throughout their lives. We pray for our forbears, for every soul who has died in the faith, and we too desire to have our share of that prayer, as long as the world shall last. Indifference to the needs of the dead is indeed tantamount to a sin, and it ought to trouble our conscience.

The relations which exist, directly or indirectly, between all men are vehicles of the imperfections common to all; it is our desire that at least within the Church these relations, which endure beyond death, should be no less inevitably vehicles of forgiveness mutually sought and granted, the prayer of all for all, so that God may pardon all.

This is an essential element in the catholicity of the Church. In this prayer of all for all, this penitence undertaken by all on behalf of all, the Church is continually being cleansed. The purity or the holiness of the Church is a dynamic aspect of her life. Sinners are not separated from the Church, nor has she any members who are without sin; all are taken up into this movement of purification through penitence, through the mutual exchange of forgiveness, through the prayer addressed to God by all that all may be forgiven. The Church is not a static society, fixed in immobility, but a dynamic communion made up of men and women who are sinners and who, at the same time, are being cleansed by their prayer for one another—not from 'sin' in the abstract, but from their actual sins, their imperfect deeds and the indifference they have shown towards particular persons.

In this living family infirmities are always apparent, but they are overcome, washed away in the ocean of mutual love between the members. All commit sin, but all contribute to the work of purification; by asking for forgiveness, by granting forgiveness, through their common interchange of prayer for the forgiveness of all. Sin is never allowed to harden into a permanent state. Those who have sinned cannot remain indifferent, they are impelled to seek forgiveness. Their conscience, quickened by the Holy Spirit, drives them to ask for it. And indeed, no sooner is it asked for than penitence begins to undo their sin. Sin is dissolved by the ceaseless waves of forgiveness, of prayer, of love, which the Holy Spirit sets in motion.

In this, all are seen to be moved by the Holy Spirit in whom they are united. The Holy Spirit is the agent of that interpersonal life which is tending towards purity, and which is incompatible with rigid, unbending patterns of relationship within the Church. He is the Spirit of freedom, of relationships formed in the freedom of love, and therefore he cannot accommodate himself to hardness, to fixed attitudes of defiance or aloofness which are produced and maintained by the pride that neither asks nor grants forgiveness. Where the passions are in control, despite their apparently fluctuating nature, a spirit of intransigence prevails, a rigidity, a constraint which only the Holy Spirit can soften and bend; and this he does when he inspires men to forgive and to ask forgiveness by rising above their pride and their other selfish passions.

This mutual forgiveness, together with the intercession of each for all, does not merely annul sin; positively, it represents the living breath of love which opens men's hearts to one another. When we speak of the breath of the Spirit, we mean that he is the bringer of love and life and freedom. True freedom is one with love, and where love is, there is goodness itself, the source of every good thought, every good word and action. There is that life which is dynamic, at the service of all, free from all bondage to pride and selfish passions.

Thus the Church is renewed through the Holy Spirit by mutual forgiveness and prayer. She is constantly renewing herself, repairing the inner bonds of love between her members. In other words, she is re-creating her inner unity, her harmony and catholicity.

The inability of Christians to bear the burden of their guilt towards others, their need to seek and to grant forgiveness, reveal the Church's inherent capacity for purification and for the continual restoration of her unity and inner bonds. So the Church becomes as it were a symphony for Christ, and so she reveals the mystery of her continuity and the mystery of the perpetual renewal of her youth.

FAIRACRES PUBLICATIONS

Complete List

No.		Price
1	RECONCILIATION Gilbert Shaw	.05
2	ALONENESS NOT LONELINESS Mother Mary Clare SLG	.05
4	INTERCESSION Mother Mary Clare SLG	.10
8	PRAYER (Devotional) Gilbert Shaw	.20
12	LEARNING TO PRAY Mother Mary Clare SLG	.20
14	STATIONS OF THE CROSS Donald McChesney	.20
15	DEATH THE GATEWAY TO LIFE Gilbert Shaw	.15
16	THE VICTORY OF THE CROSS Dumitru Staniloae	.20
21	THE THEOLOGY OF THE RELIGIOUS LIFE A.M. Allchin	.20
23	THE APOSTOLATE OF PRAYER Mother Mary Clare SLG	.20
24	SILENCE AND PRAYER Mother Mary Clare SLG	.20
26	THE MESSAGE OF ST SERAPHIM Irina Gorainov	.30
28	JULIAN OF NORWICH A.M. Allchin and SLG	.50
31	PRAYER: ENCOUNTERING THE DEPTHS Mother Mary Clare SLG	.20
32	THE CONTEMPLATIVE LIFE: A Current Approach, Sr Eileen Mary SLG	.20
34	LITURGY TODAY: Divine Office and Eucharist, Sr Benedicta SLG	.30
35	THE WORD OF GOD: Reading the Bible, Sr Mary Paul SLG	.15
36	EXPLORING SILENCE Wendy Robinson	.30
37	LEISURE Mother Mary Clare SLG	.10
39	THE CHRISTIAN CONCEPT OF SACRIFICE Michael Ramsey	.10
40	ST THERESE OF LISIEUX: Her Relevance for Today, Sr Eileen Mary SLG	.20
43	THE POWER OF THE NAME: The Jesus Prayer in Orthodox Spirituality, Kallistos Ware	.35
46	PRAYER AND CONTEMPLATION Robert Llewelyn	£1.50
48	THE WISDOM OF THE DESERT FATHERS trans. Sr Benedicta SLG	£1.50
50	THE LETTERS OF ST ANTONY THE GREAT trans. Derwas J. Chitty	.50
54	FROM LONELINESS TO SOLITUDE Roland Walls	.10
55	THEOLOGY AND SPIRITUALITY Andrew Louth	.35
60	THE INFLUENCE OF ST BERNARD Anglican Essays with an Introduction by Jean Leclercq OSB. Edited by Sr Benedicta SLG	£1.75
61	KABIR: THE WAY OF LOVE AND PARADOX Sr Rosemary SLG	.35
63	EVELYN UNDERHILL Two Centenary Essays, Michael Ramsey and A.M. Allchin	.35
64	TOWARDS CONTEMPLATION A Practical Introduction for Prayer Groups, Peter Dodson	.30
65	THE POSITIVE ROLE OF DISTRACTION IN PRAYER Robert Llewelyn	.15
66	SOLITUDE AND COMMUNION Papers on the Hermit Life by Orthodox Catholic and Anglican contributors. Edited by A.M. Allchin	£1.50
67	MARY AND THE MYSTERY OF THE INCARNATION An Essay on the Mother of God in the Theology of Karl Barth, Andrew Louth	.30